BLACKBERRY BRAMBLE

A bramble is any prickly shrub or vine. Blackberry brambles often grow wild along fences, in woods, and in unplowed fields.

A COW'S DAILY LIFE

Dairy cows are milked twice each day, morning and evening. At some dairy farms, cows are confined all day. At others, they are free to move about as they please between milkings. In warm weather they may go out to pasture. In cold weather, they may rest in a loafing barn, a shed with only three sides. Cows eat 40 to 60 pounds of food each day, including grain, hay, chopped-up corn stalks, and plants growing in the pasture. They drink 10 to 20 gallons of water each day. Cows sleep at night on a bed of straw or sawdust. In summer, they may sleep outdoors.

COWBIRD

The cowbird is a kind of blackbird. It likes to spend time around cattle because of the insects they stir up. Sometimes cowbirds actually help cattle by picking ticks and insects off their hides.

CUD

A cow's stomach has four compartments. Food is first gulped down with very little chewing. After juices in the first compartment soften the food, it is drawn back into the cow's mouth. The cow rechews this cud, then swallows it for further digestion in the other stomach compartments. A cow spends several hours a day quietly chewing its cud. We sometimes say that a person lost in thought is "chewing the cud."

MILK

Milk is the most nourishing of all foods. It is an outstanding source of the nutrients required for growth and body maintenance—carbohydrates, fats, minerals, proteins, and vitamins. Milk comes in many forms: whole milk, 1% and 2% milk, skim milk, buttermilk, evaporated, condensed, and dry milk. Most milk drunk in the U.S. comes from cows, but in other countries people drink milk from goats, water buffalo, sheep, reindeer, camels, and llamas.

BREEDS OF DAIRY COWS

There are six major breeds of dairy cows in the U.S. Holsteins, the largest and most common, are black and white. Guernsey cows are smaller and are red, fawn, or brown with white patches. Other breeds are Ayrshire, Brown Swiss, Jersey, and Milking Shorthorn.

MILKING MACHINE

Almost all cows in the U.S. are milked with a milking machine. The machine attaches to the cow's teats and pumps the milk either into a nearby container or by pipeline directly to a cooling tank in a separate milk house. From there the milk is pumped into tank trucks for delivery to the processing plant. The old-fashioned 10-gallon milk can is almost a thing of the past.

OTHER DAIRY PRODUCTS

Many other dairy products are made from milk, including butter, cheese, sour cream, yogurt, and ice cream.

Juv/F
T   29252

Talley, Carol

Clarissa

CLARISSA

Written by **Carol Talley**

Illustrated by **Itoko Maeno**

MarshMedia, Kansas City, Missouri

To Penny Paine,
who conceived of Clarissa's story

Special thanks to Dawn Jax Belleau, Mindy Bingham, Lin Closing, Bud Dean, Marilyn Faulkner, Charles Hammer, Jim Knight, Julitta Langle, Jane Maas, Alan Marsh, Betty Shepperd, Sandy Stryker, Linda Talley, Karen Thompson, and Michael Jones Thompson.

Text copyright © 1992 by Marsh Film Enterprises, Inc.
Illustrations copyright © 1992 by Itoko Maeno

Published by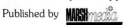

A Division of Marsh Film Enterprises, Inc.
P.O. Box 8082
Shawnee Mission, KS 66208

Library of Congress Cataloging-in-Publication Data

Talley, Carol

　　Clarissa

　　　　Summary: Clarissa, a plain brown cow who allows herself to be pushed around by all the other animals on her Wisconsin farm, helps a group of lost domestic animals find their way to the fair and demonstrates that she is bright, brave, and creative. Includes factual information on Wisconsin, farm life, dairy products, and fairs.

　　　　[1. Cows—Fiction. 2. Farm life—Fiction. 3. Fairs—Fiction. 4. Self-respect—Fiction. 5. Wisconsin—Fiction.] I. Paine, Penelope Colville, 1946-　　. II. Maeno, Itoko, ill. III. Title.
PZ7.T15635Cl 1992　　　　[Fic]　　　　91-29958
ISBN 1-55942-014-6

Book layout by Christine Nolt

Printed in USA

Mmmmmooo-ve over, Clarissa," demanded Fiona. "I want some of those blackberries, too." Fiona was a big black and white Holstein and—Clarissa was sure—the bossiest cow in Wisconsin.

"Oh, Clarissa," said Tessy, "I bet you found these sweet, juicy berries just for me! But I must have more room, dear." Tessy was a beautiful brown and white Guernsey and very self-centered. Now Clarissa couldn't reach any blackberries at all for herself.

Fiona and Tessy were always pushing Clarissa around. They nudged her away from the sweet patches of clover she found. They crowded her from the shade of the old oak tree. They shoved ahead of her at the feeding trough.

But Clarissa never complained. It seemed to her that you had to be big and bossy like Fiona or beautiful like Tessy to get what you wanted. And she was neither. Clarissa was just a plain brown cow.

Early each morning, Fiona, Tessy, Clarissa, and the other cows on the Larson dairy farm were milked by Mr. Larson and his son Pete.

Through the long summer
mornings, the herd grazed in
the far pasture, settling down in the
afternoons to chew their cud. No one
dared disturb Fiona as she thought her bossy
thoughts or Tessy as she gazed at her pretty
reflection in the water. But things
were different for Clarissa.

The sheepdog ran circles around her, pretending she was a flock of unruly sheep.

The noisy cowbirds hitched rides on her broad, strong back as she ambled across the pasture.

And pesky bluebottle flies swarmed around her patient brow. There was little time for Clarissa to think her own thoughts or dream her own dreams.

In the evening, when it was again time for milking, Fiona led the way back to the barnyard. Tessy came behind her, always careful to keep her dainty hooves clean. Clarissa followed, even though she was clever enough to find her own way home.

Mr. Larson greeted the cows as they came through the gate. "Good job," he praised Fiona. "Hello, my beauty," he welcomed pretty Tessy. "Get a move on, old girl," he said as he swatted Clarissa on the rump. Clarissa wished that, just once, *she* could be the special cow, praised instead of pushed around. But she moved obligingly through the barnyard gate.

Pete, at least, was kind to her. "Clarissa is such a smart cow," he told his father. "And she is so good and gentle."

"I'd rather be beautiful," thought Tessy.

"I'd rather be boss," thought Fiona.

One hot August morning, when the hay had been mowed and baled and the corn was sky high, the usually quiet dirt road running past the Larson farm came alive. Through the dust, Clarissa could see loads of lumber and bright canvas, bouncing pigs and chickens, wide-eyed horses and cows, all disappearing up the neighboring lane and over the hill.

"Stop that commotion!" bawled Fiona.

"My beautiful coat is getting dirty," worried Tessy.

Clarissa watched in silence. She was remembering other Augusts, when the tassels on the tall corn turned brown in the sun and the road became a cloud of dust.

"It's the fair!" she whispered to herself.

The next morning, right after the milking, Pete hauled out hoses and buckets of soapy water and bathed Fiona and Tessy. He brushed their coats and combed their tails. As his father polished their hooves, Pete braided a yellow ribbon into Tessy's tail and hung a shiny brass cowbell around Fiona's neck. "I think Tessy and Fiona are going to win ribbons this year," Mr. Larson said.

"I hope so, Dad. But what about Clarissa? Can't she go to the fair too?"

"It takes something special to win a ribbon, Pete. And Clarissa's as ordinary as her plain brown cow face. She's just not the kind of cow that gets taken to the fair."

Later that morning, alone in the far pasture, Clarissa stared into the pond and grew angry at the face she saw reflected there. "Why can't you be more like Fiona and Tessy?" she asked herself. She didn't want to be bossy and stuck-up like them. But she did want others to look up to her. She wanted to be loved. And she wanted to go to the fair. "I'll never be anything but the last cow through the barnyard gate," she said. Two big tears rolled down her soft nose and plopped into the water.

Just then, Clarissa heard a small voice.

"Maybe we should ask her to help us."

Turning her head, Clarissa saw a rooster, a duck, a floppy-eared rabbit, a goat, and a huge red-and-white-spotted pig.

"How could she help us?" snorted the pig. "Look at her! She's nothing but a plain old brown cow."

The other animals ignored him.

"We ran away from the fair," said the rooster.

"We've been playing all night," chimed in the duck.

"We have to get back for the competition," cried the goat.

"But we're lost!" wailed the floppy-eared rabbit.

"Oh, I'll get us back," said the pig. "Just give me time to think!"

Clarissa was tempted to let him try. "I should just let him get everyone hopelessly lost," she said to herself. "If I can't go to the fair, why should they?" But Clarissa knew that helping would be the right thing to do. "I certainly know the way," she thought. "And, this once at least, everyone would be following *me*."

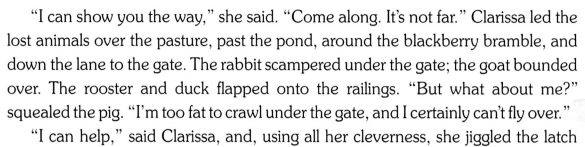

"I can show you the way," she said. "Come along. It's not far." Clarissa led the lost animals over the pasture, past the pond, around the blackberry bramble, and down the lane to the gate. The rabbit scampered under the gate; the goat bounded over. The rooster and duck flapped onto the railings. "But what about me?" squealed the pig. "I'm too fat to crawl under the gate, and I certainly can't fly over."

"I can help," said Clarissa, and, using all her cleverness, she jiggled the latch with her nose until the gate slid open and the pig pushed through.

"I can see the pennants!" cried the rooster. "We're almost there!"

The happy animals started up the last hill toward the fair, and Clarissa began to shut the gate. Then she stopped. Being helpful and being smart had brought her this far, but this wasn't far enough. She wanted to go to the fair too. Even if she was just an ordinary cow. Even if Fiona and Tessy laughed to see her there. Even if Mr. Larson was very angry. "Maybe sometimes," she thought, "you just have to be brave and go after what you want."

"Wait for me!" she called out.

"I'M GOING TO THE FAIR TOO!"

The animals turned in their tracks. "Hurrah!" shouted the rabbit. "Hurrah!" shouted all the lost-and-found animals.

"You lead the way, Clarissa," said the pig. And the little band waddled, hopped, walked and flapped its way up the hill.

Meanwhile, there was consternation at the fair.

"Where can my duck be?" cried a freckle-faced girl.

"And who has got my goat?" asked someone else.

"I'll give a fat reward to anyone who can find my prize pig," said a man in overalls.

Just then, Mr. Larson and Pete looked up and saw Clarissa coming over the ridge of the hill. "What's she doing here?" exclaimed Mr. Larson. "As if we didn't have enough problems!"

But the next instant, the rabbit, the duck, the rooster, the goat, and the pig trooped over the hill behind Clarissa.

"Clarissa found the lost animals," shouted Pete, "and she's led them back where they belong!"

Finally Clarissa was at the fair. And what sights she saw! Striped tents, banners, and balloons. The midway, the merry-go-round, and the giant Ferris wheel. She breathed in the wonderful smells of hay and fruit pies and farm animals and tractor engines. She heard the burst of fireworks and the music of the calliope. Then she heard her own name.

As Clarissa turned, a little girl slipped a garland of daisies around her neck. "Hooray for Clarissa!" shouted the crowd that had gathered around her. "This is your blue-ribbon day!" proclaimed the pig.

"You've always been smart and you've always been good," Pete told Clarissa. "Today, you proved that you are also strong and brave and adventurous. Welcome to the fair!"

But that's not the end of Clarissa's story.

One day, when summer was over and Mr. Larson was thinking seriously about bringing in the corn, he received a visit from a Mr. A.J. Nettleford. "I've been looking for a cow," Mr. Nettleford said, "a very special cow." Fiona and Tessy looked up expectantly.

"This cow will help me promote good health, along with all my dairy products. So, you see, she has to be more than just another pretty face," he said, passing by Tessy. "And I don't want one of those bossy cows either." He looked sharply at Fiona. "I want a cow that's bright and brave and creative. She should be easy to get along with, but not afraid to stand up for herself. I've heard from folks around here that you might have such a cow."

"I'll say," said Pete. "That description fits Clarissa to a T!"

And that's how Clarissa became famous. That's how her plain but good and intelligent face came to be on billboards, on milk cartons, and on the shiny Nettleford Dairy trucks that travel all over Wisconsin.

Clarissa's success did not really change life on the Larson farm. Fiona was still bossy, and Tessy was still self-centered, and Clarissa continued to tolerate them with her good-natured patience. But she never again thought of herself as an ordinary cow . . .

Clarissa knew she was a winner, and
she saw more blue-ribbon days ahead.

Dear Parents and Educators:

Every child wants to be special—to be loved and looked up to. Children who have learned to appreciate their inherent worth and to recognize, develop, and use their special abilities have the means to achieve this wish.

But many, like Clarissa, are uncertain how to gain the love and respect of others. They may not be convinced that they are worthy of esteem. They may doubt that they have special abilities. They may worry that if they value themselves too highly they will be vain Tessys, or that if they place importance on their own needs they will be bossy Fionas.

A challenge facing parents and teachers is to help children recognize their value to themselves and to others, to provide opportunities for the exploration and development of their talents, and to encourage positive risk-taking in the achievement of goals.

To help children understand the message of *Clarissa*, discuss the following questions with them:

- At the beginning of the story, what opinion did Clarissa have of herself?

- How did it seem to Clarissa that Fiona and Tessy were able to get what they wanted?

- What things did Pete admire about Clarissa?

- Why wasn't Clarissa taken to the fair?

- What did Clarissa prove about herself by deciding to go to the fair?

- How did things change for Clarissa after the fair?

- What are some qualities that make you special?

- What is something you would like to accomplish?

- When have you had to be brave and stand up for yourself?

Here are some ways you can help children recognize their worth and take active steps to achieve their goals and dreams:

- Teach children to appreciate the inherent worth of each person.

- Help children identify their personal strengths and abilities.

- Provide opportunities for children to develop and use their special talents and abilities.

- Stress that fulfilling dreams requires more than talent; it requires action and sometimes courage.

- Be a positive role model for risk-taking in the achievement of goals.

- Emphasize that acting responsibly toward others does not require denial of one's own needs.

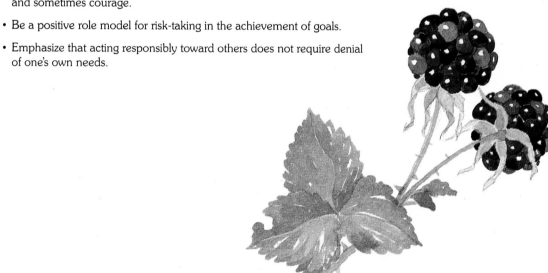

Available from MarshMedia

The following are six very special storybooks; six videos blending winning narration, music, sound effects, and Itoko Maeno's watercolors; and six activity books full of games, puzzles, maps, and project ideas for one child or a classroom of children.

Clarissa, written by Carol Talley, illustrated by Itoko Maeno. Hardcover with dust jacket, 32 pages with full-color illustrations throughout. (MarshMedia) ISBN 1-55942-014-6. $15.95.

Clarissa video, based on the book written by Carol Talley and illustrated by Itoko Maeno. 13:00 run time. (MarshMedia) ISBN 1-55942-023-5. $59.95.

Clarissa activity book. Softcover, 24 pages. (MarshMedia) ISBN 1-55942-024-3. $14.95.

Kylie's Song, written by Patty Sheehan, illustrated by Itoko Maeno. Hardcover with dust jacket, 32 pages with full-color illustrations throughout. (Advocacy Press) ISBN 0-911655-19-0. $16.95.

Kylie's Song video, based on the book written by Patty Sheehan and illustrated by Itoko Maeno. 12:00 run time. (MarshMedia) ISBN 1-55942-021-9. $59.95.

Kylie's Song activity book. Softcover, 28 pages. (MarshMedia) ISBN 1-55942-022-7. $14.95.

Minou, written by Mindy Bingham, illustrated by Itoko Maeno. Hardcover with dust jacket, 64 pages with full-color illustrations throughout. (Advocacy Press) ISBN 0-911655-36-0. $14.95.

Minou video, based on the book written by Mindy Bingham and illustrated by Itoko Maeno. 18:30 run time. (MarshMedia) ISBN 1-55942-015-4. $59.95.

Minou activity book. Softcover, 24 pages. (MarshMedia) ISBN 1-55942-016-2. $14.95.

My Way Sally, written by Mindy Bingham and Penelope Paine, illustrated by Itoko Maeno. Hardcover with dust jacket, 48 pages with full-color illustrations throughout. (Advocacy Press) ISBN 0-911655-27-1. $13.95.

My Way Sally video, based on the book written by Mindy Bingham and Penelope Paine and illustrated by Itoko Maeno. 19:30 run time. (MarshMedia) ISBN 1-55942-017-0. $59.95.

My Way Sally activity book. Softcover, 24 pages. (MarshMedia) ISBN 1-55942-018-9. $14.95.

Time for Horatio, written by Penelope Paine, illustrated by Itoko Maeno. Hardcover with dust jacket, 48 pages with full-color illustrations throughout. (Advocacy Press) ISBN 0-911655-33-6. $14.95.

Time for Horatio video, based on the book written by Penelope Paine and illustrated by Itoko Maeno. 19:00 run time. (MarshMedia) ISBN 1-55942-026-X. $59.95.

Time for Horatio activity book. Softcover, 24 pages. (MarshMedia) ISBN 1-55942-027-8. $14.95.

Tonia the Tree, written by Sandy Stryker, illustrated by Itoko Maeno. Hardcover with dust jacket, 32 pages with full-color illustrations throughout. (Advocacy Press) ISBN 0-911655-16-6. $13.95.

Tonia the Tree video, based on the book written by Sandy Stryker and illustrated by Itoko Maeno. 12:10 run time. (MarshMedia) ISBN 1-55942-019-7. $59.95.

Tonia the Tree activity book. Softcover, 20 pages. (MarshMedia) ISBN 1-55942-020-0. $14.95.

You can find these storybooks at better bookstores. Or you may order storybooks, videos, and activity books direct by sending a check for the amount shown plus $3.50 for shipping to MarshMedia, P.O. Box 8082, Shawnee Mission, Kansas 66208, or by calling 1-800-821-3303.

MarshMedia has been publishing high-quality, award-winning learning materials for children since 1969. To receive a catalog, call 1-800-821-3303.

FAIRS

Fairs are celebrations of farm life and harvest time. They include carnival rides and sideshows; livestock, produce, craft and homemaking competitions; demonstrations of farm equipment and of skills such as sheep-shearing and milking; and special events such as greased-pig contests, balloon ascensions, and sometimes a rodeo.

FERRIS WHEEL

The Ferris wheel was invented by George Ferris for Chicago's Columbian Exposition in 1893. Most Ferris wheels today are about 50 feet in diameter, but this first one soared 250 feet above the ground. The largest Ferris wheel ever erected was in London. It stood 328 feet high and could carry 1200 passengers.

MIDWAY

The term midway, first used at the Columbian Exposition in Chicago in 1893, refers to the avenue at a fair where sideshows, carnival rides, and refreshment stands are located.

MERRY-GO-ROUND

Merry-go-rounds, also called carousels, have been operated in the U.S. since the eighteenth century. Brightly painted benches or animals—often horses—revolve on a platform, usually to the sound of music.

WISCONSIN

Although its official nickname is the Badger State, Wisconsin is also called the Dairy State and America's Dairyland. Wisconsin has more cows and produces more milk, butter, and cheese than any other state. The name Wisconsin comes from the Indian term meaning "Gathering of the Waters," and the state has 10,000 miles of rivers and more than 8,000 lakes. Wisconsin's state flower is the wood violet and the state bird is the robin.

HAY

Hay, the dried stems and leaves of plants such as alfalfa, clover, or certain grasses, is used as feed for animals. Farmers cut the hay, dry it, and bale it. Baling machines gather hay into large bundles and tie them with wire or twine.

CALLIOPE

The calliope is a keyboard instrument similar to an organ. The piercing notes of its steam whistles can be heard for more than 10 miles, so it is perfect for drawing crowds to a fair or circus. Invented in 1855, the calliope is a rare sight today.

CORN

There are several kinds of corn: the sweet corn we eat off the cob; popcorn; a type of hard corn that is ground into corn meal to make cornbread and tortillas; and field corn, which is used mostly to feed livestock. Field corn may grow 10 feet tall. The tassels on corn turn dark when it is ready to pick.